PHOTOGRAPHIC MEMORIES

OF

SCOTLAND

Front cover picture:
Edinburgh Castle viewed from Grassmarket, 1897

Above:
Iona Abbey, Iona, 1903

FRANCIS FRITH & HIS UNIQUE ARCHIVE

In 1860, Francis Frith, the Quaker son of a Chesterfield cooper, was 38 years old. He had already sold a massive grocery business he had built up, for a small fortune. Like Livingstone and Stanley, Frith was fired with a romantic wanderlust, and the Victorian deep passion for travelling and exploring. Between 1857 and '59 he made several pioneering photographic journeys to remote regions of the Nile that brought him considerable fame.

After his marriage in 1860, he confined his wanderings a little closer to home and began a series of photo trips around Britain. His aim was to make his pictures available to the greatest number of people possible - life was hard and drab for millions of Victorians, and Frith believed his 'view souvenirs' of seaside resorts, beauty spots and town and village scenes would help keep their rare days out alive in their memories. He was right: by 1890 he had created the largest photographic publishing company in the world!

As well as thousands of views of high streets around Britain, Frith's growing archive included beautiful scenes of leafy glades, dusty lanes, rocks and coastlines, and the boats and riversides, beloved of Victorian wanderers like Jerome K Jerome - whose 'Three Men in a Boat' had struck a strong chord with the public.

Life in the Frith family was never dull. The family went with him on many trips, and the highlights were recorded by his wife, Mary Ann, in her journal. In 1872 she tells of a relaxing three week expedition to Ilfracombe in North Devon. Whilst such trips may have been something of a holiday for his wife and children, Francis Frith found no time to put his feet up. He was up and down the coast photographing Barnstaple and Lynton, hiring carters to carry him out to remote locations, and boatmen to row him round the bay to view and photograph spectacular cliff formations.

After Francis Frith died in 1898 his sons carried on the business for many years with great success, specialising in postcards and other prints. So impressive is the archive he started that **The Financial Times** called it '*a unique and priceless record of English life in the last century*'.

PHOTOGRAPHIC MEMORIES

OF

SCOTLAND

THE FRANCIS FRITH COLLECTION

This edition published by
The Francis Frith Collection exclusively for
Selecta Books Ltd., Roundway, Devizes,
Wiltshire SN10 2HR
in association with Michael Brewer.

First published 1995

© The Francis Frith Collection

ISBN 1 85937 017 9

Printed in Singapore

The Francis Frith Collection
The Old Rectory, Bimport, Shaftesbury, Dorset SP7 8AT
Tel: 01747 855669 Fax: 01747 855065

Contents

MELROSE. Nestling between the Tweed and the Eildon Hills, the pretty town of Melrose, with its narrow streets and pretty cottages is as delightful to today's visitors as it was to those in Frith's day. The romantic ruins of Melrose Abbey, steeped in history, rise majestically above the town.

Right: Market Place and Old Cross, Melrose, 1897. Further up the street we come to the Market Place, the focal point for all trade as well as a meeting point for the locals on market day. In the doorway stands a man with an obvious interest in the photographer, somewhat of a novelty in 1897.

Below: Melrose square, 1901. With the Eildon hills in the background, this is a lovely view of the quaint town of Melrose with its charming, narrow, cobbled streets. On the right can be seen the 'Anderson's Temperance Hotel',whilst outside some little girls can be seen in their charming pinafore dresses..

Right: Melrose Abbey, 1897. Rumour has it that the heart of Robert the Bruce is buried here in the picturesque and romantic ruins of Melrose Abbey. The Abbey, with its beautiful pink tinted stone, dominates its gorgeous riverside surroundings.

Below: Abbotsford House, 1890. Here we have a beautiful view of the house that was built for Sir Walter Scott. The Gillie, in his boat on the river Tweed is checking his stretch of water for the start of the fishing season.

MOFFAT is a delightful market town with some fine Georgian architecture, reminiscent of its brief period of glory as a fashionable spa in the eighteenth century, owing to its sulphur springs. The Victorians enjoyed its aspect, but not its waters.

Right: The Fountain, Moffat, c 1890. The bronze ram statue on the Colvin fountain was erected in the middle of the town square to comemorate Moffat's origins in the wool trade. The most notable feature is that it was accidentally cast without ears!

Below: The Old and New Bridges of Dumfries, 1890. The 'Auld Brig' seen here is a lovely footbridge spanning the River Nith. Originally built in the 1432 but restored after flood damage in the 17th century.

Top: Moffat High Street, 1890. A busy view of the high street that boasts a combination of grand Georgian Mansions and simple brick cottages. In the 18th century Moffat was, for a short while, a spa town, and was described by one visitor as smelling of bilge-water. **Below: Tennis Court, Moffat, 1892.** A lively game of tennis draws a lot of spectators.

AYR. In bygone days Ayr was a thriving seaport, but later developed as a market town. The Victorians made it a popular resort - the new town of wide, elegant streets was behind the beach, southwest of the old town.

Twa Brigs, Ayr, 1900. The Auld Brig, made famous by Robert Burns in his poem of the same name, stretches across the River Ayr. This beautiful old cobbled relic of medieval times stands along side the new bridge built in the Victorian era.

Sandgate Street, Ayr, 1900. Looking down towards the new bridge, the Auld Kirk rises majestically above Ayr. The church was funded by Cromwell as he had taken over the previous kirk into his stronghold. Many friends of Burns are buried in the graveyard.

Top: Twa Brigs, Ayr, 1900. A splendid scene with the river Ayr being spanned by the stately 'Twa Brigs of Ayr' and the "Auld Kirk" rising majestically on the left. **Below: Ayr High Street, 1900.** A barefooted delivery boy returns from his errand while the shopkeeper peers out of Mr McLean's tinsmith shop. On the opposite side of the street a small group gathers outside Ritchie & Co which is advertising Ice Cream and Fried Fish.

GLASGOW, the centre of working class industrial Scotland, grew up around the shipbuilding industry on the Clyde and other heavy industries that evolved from the technologically developing Industrial Revolution. Later in the 1930's, the swift moving tide of the country's financial troubles created the great Depression. This caused terrible hardship and unemployment to the hard-working people of Glasgow living in the slum tenements of the Gorbals.

Right: The Broomielaw, Glasgow, 1897. These docks were made famous by being the main disembarking point for the potato pickers who came over from from Ireland .

St. Vincent Place, Glasgow, 1897. Glasgow has some of the finest examples of Victorian architecture as is evident in the splendid buildings in this photograph. The fine figure of the policeman seems to be almost modern compared with the heavily clad pedestrians.

Above: Broomielaw, 1897. An excellent overhead view of the Broomielaw area of Glasgow with the George V bridge in the foreground. The ships can be seen tied up at the quay waiting to load up with cargo and passengers for the Clyde coastal resorts.

Left: Cathedral & Necropolis, Glasgow, 1890. Set on the outer edge of the city this beautiful cathedral with interesting architectural features such as its stumpy spire stands as a proud reminder of the 'birth' of Glasgow'.

Above: The Royal Exchange, Glasgow, 1897. This imposing building, where the merchants of Glasgow grew rich on the trading of tobacco and sugar imported from America, is a traditional meeting place for business men.

Below: George Square, Glasgow, 1897. Looking down from his eighty foot high column, Sir Walter Scott surveys the bustle of George Square. Whilst some people stroll around the square others hurry across the road to avoid being run down by a tram. Horses pulling carts loaded down with cargo seem oblivious to the noise of the trams and motor cars around them.
Opposite: Renfield Street, Glasgow, 1897. Overlooked by the Lancashire Insurance Building, this busy street has all manner of tradesmen and professionals going about their business.

Top: Glasgow University, 1897. Designed by Sir Gilbert Scott in the mid-nineteenth century, it was a comparatively new edifice when this photograph was taken. The pride of Victorians, it seems rather forbidding to the modern eye.
Below: Glasgow Stock Exchange, 1897. A fine example of the Victorian penchant for mixing styles, the gothic overtones are much in evidence.

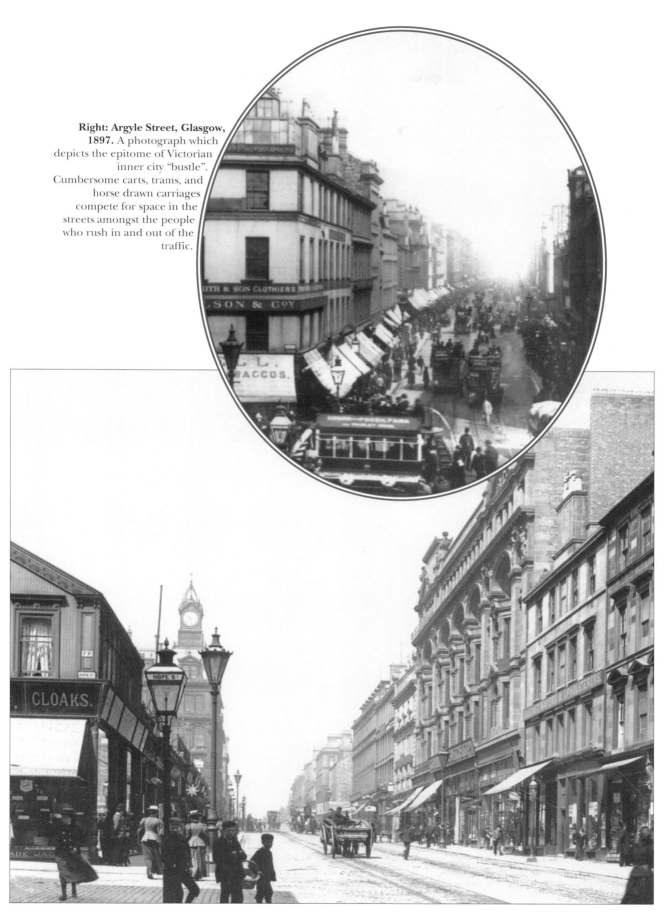

Right: Argyle Street, Glasgow, 1897. A photograph which depicts the epitome of Victorian inner city "bustle". Cumbersome carts, trams, and horse drawn carriages compete for space in the streets amongst the people who rush in and out of the traffic.

Above: Sauchiehall Street, Glasgow, 1897. This famous street, in the commercial heart of Glasgow, and is one of the long straight roads which form part of the distinctive grid system in this area. John Betjamin called this area *"the greatest Victorian city in the world"* This street is now for pedestrians only, and is one of the premier shopping streets in Glasgow.

CLYDEBANK, known and respected world wide as the centre of Scottish shipbuilding and the 'Second City of the Empire', once produced such nautical gems as the QEII and the Royal Yacht Britannia. Today, unfortunately, this is not to be. Years of unemployment and recession have taken their toll on the town leaving and it is now a shadow of its former self.

Right: Glasgow Road, Clydebank, 1900. In its heyday, Clydebank was a flourishing, hectic place to live, populated by hardworking, hard drinking, labourers employed by the famous yards such as John Brown & Co.

Below: Glasgow Road, Clydebank, c 1900. Pedestrians, under the watchful eye of a policeman, wait for the tram to pass before crossing Glasgow Road.

Above: Kilbowie Road, Clydebank, 1900. A busy crossing point not made any easier by the horse and cart obstructing the bridge. Note the house side plastered with advertisements for products such as Colmans Starch and Camp Coffee.

Left: Town Hall under construction, Clydebank, 1900. A holiday parade in Clydebank attracts hundreds of spectators, but the workmen building the new town hall have the best view.

P AISLEY is best known for its swirling pine cone design textiles which evolved from the production of imitation Kashmiri shawls. The original shawls were brought back by soldiers returning from serving in India and were then adapted by the towns people.

Left: County Buildings, Paisley, 1900.

Above: Paisley High Street, 1900. A rainy day in Paisley. Note the fine examples of Victorian ironwork, particularly in the street lamps. The five-stage spire of the High Church is a memorable landmark against the skyline in the background.

Above: Dunn Square, Paisley, 1901. Children play around the statue, while their elders 'take the air' and stroll or sit in the sun.

Above: Dunn Square, Paisley, 1897. With its unusual, mismatched towers, the Town Hall looms over Dunn Square where the tidy walkways fan out like the spokes of a wheel. It faces over the river rather than the town.

Above: Graham Street, Barrhead, c 1918.
Children play on the the street corner
outside the Barrhead Co-Operative
Society as a motor car makes its way down
the hill.

Left: Barrhead, c 1890. An earlier view of
Barrhead shows the main form of
transport to be horse and carriage, as this
immaculately turned out pair drive past
Shanks & Co. the famous manufacturers
of sanitary porcelain that was exported all
over the world.

GREENOCK was the site of the first dock built on the river Clyde. Soon a thriving ship building industry grew which spread along the banks of the Clyde. Unfortunately this great industry suffered under the onslaught of the Great Depression.

Right: Princes Pier, Greenock, 1904. A steam ferry departs from the pier. Maybe taking holiday makers to Dunoon and Rothesay.

Above: Customs House Quay, Greenock, 1897. Outside the offices of the Glasgow, Dublin & Londonderry Steam Packet Company people await the arrival of a steamer coming down the Clyde. In the background can be seen the famous shipyards of the Clyde which were the mainstay of Scottish industry for many years.

Top: Yachts on the Clyde, 1897. Surrounded by yachts bobbing on the water, the steam cruiser, bedecked in flags and bunting, makes its way on a pleasure trip down the Clyde.**Below: Ardgowan Bowling Green, Greenock, 1904.** Residents of Greenock enjoy an afternoon game of bowls.**Opposite: Greenock Harbour, 1904.** Standing at 245 feet this Victorian tower dominates Greenock's skyline.

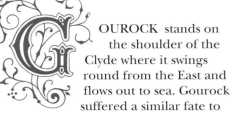

GOUROCK stands on the shoulder of the Clyde where it swings round from the East and flows out to sea. Gourock suffered a similar fate to Glasgow and Greenock during the depression in the 1930's as its main industry was also shipbuilding. The "Tail of the Bank", as it was known, was where the larger ocean going liners would disembark their passengers for transfer to Glasgow by train.

Right: From the pier, Gourock, 1900. Rising from the deck of the steamer, the funnel towers high above the men on the quay.

Below: Gourock, 1900. A panoramic view of the shipping town of Gourock. In the distance you can see the Clyde stretching away towards Glasgow with many different kinds of boats laying at anchor.

Above: Kempock Street, Gourock, 1900. Three likely lads take a lot of interest in the photographer, but everyone else seems more interested in the shop windows.

Left: Hunters Quay, Gourock, 1897. A beautifully composed photograph. A paddle steamer chugging across the bay, with several yachts scudding across the water.

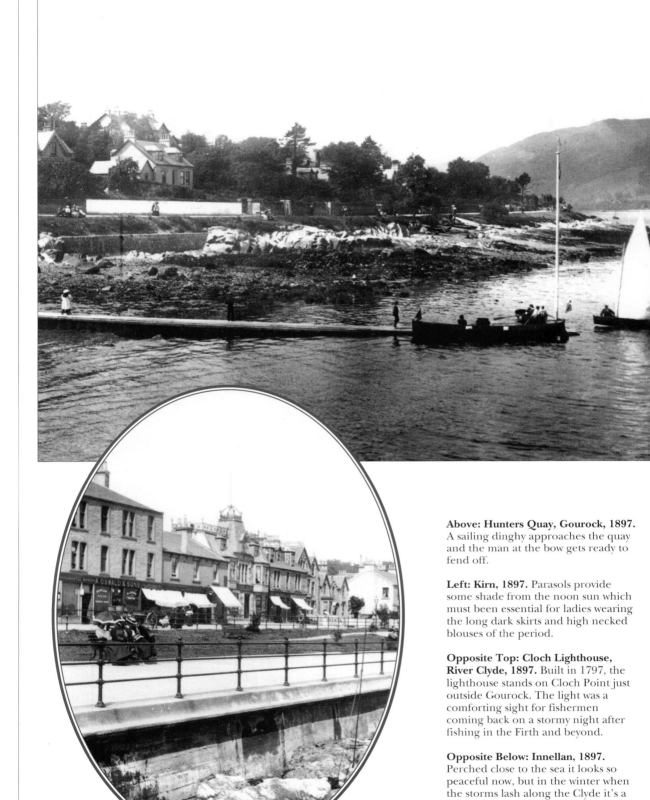

Above: Hunters Quay, Gourock, 1897. A sailing dinghy approaches the quay and the man at the bow gets ready to fend off.

Left: Kirn, 1897. Parasols provide some shade from the noon sun which must been essential for ladies wearing the long dark skirts and high necked blouses of the period.

Opposite Top: Cloch Lighthouse, River Clyde, 1897. Built in 1797, the lighthouse stands on Cloch Point just outside Gourock. The light was a comforting sight for fishermen coming back on a stormy night after fishing in the Firth and beyond.

Opposite Below: Innellan, 1897. Perched close to the sea it looks so peaceful now, but in the winter when the storms lash along the Clyde it's a very different place.

L ARGS is commonly held to be the most "agreeable" resort along the North Ayrshire coast. Set against a backdrop of rolling hills, it gained and maintained a reputation as a traditional family holiday spot - unpretentious, comfortable and attractive.

Previous page: Largs, 1897. Children enjoy a romp on the beach at Largs. It was near here that a fierce battle was once fought between the Scots and the Vikings. and even today this battle is celebrated every September.

Right: Largs, 1897. A leisurely stroll along the quay or messing around in boats is a great way of passing a lazy sunday afternoon.

Above: Millport, 1897. Low tide, and the small rowing boats bob gently at anchor in this picturesque town on an island in the Firth of Clyde near Largs. This was a popular port of call for the yachts from the Clyde Cruising Club, because of its sheltered mooring.

Top: Irvine Parish Church, 1904. This squat but imposing building with the strangely tapered tower dominates Britain first "new town by the sea. **Above: Irvine, 1904.** Once one of Glasgow's main ports, this lovely perspective view features the Winton Arms which was probably a favourite haunt for Glaswegian sailors.

UNOON sits on the Firth of Clyde looking across towards Gourock. The hills that form a backdrop to the town are covered in blue-green trees. This attractive sprawling resort is easily accessible by regular ferries from Gourock. The gardens boast the "Highland Mary" statue - Mary Campbell, Robert Burns' sweetheart.

Right: West Bay, Dunoon, 1897. Children play on the pebbly beach or paddle in the sea while their heavily clothed mothers gossip and look on in this lovely summer scene.

Above: The Pier at Dunoon, 1901. A small boat disembarks its passengers from a pleasure trip.while a little girl waits for them at the top of the steps. The pier looks much the same today.

Above: The Argyll Hotel, Dunoon, 1897.
Perched on the quay, the Argyll Hotel offers high class accommodation to the more prosperous holiday makers spending the summer at Dunoon. It is a favourite place with Glaswegians who come over on the ferry from Gourock.

Left: The Argyll Hotel, Dunoon, 1904.
Another view of the 'Argyll', but this time seen from a much higher vantage point, possibly from a church spire, shows the backdrop of hills which run round in a crescent behind the town.

ROTHESAY. The principal town of the Isle of Bute in the Firth of Clyde, was probably the most popular resort for Glaswegians, attracting a great number of people in the summer. If one walks along the coastline it is possible to see many kinds of wildlife including seals and seagulls and find lovely secluded little coves where the only noise is the sound of the waves breaking on the beach.

Previous pages: Rothesay, 1897. The only way to reach the beautiful island of Bute is by boat. Here we can see the steam ferries going back to Wemyss Bay or Gourock full of holiday makers at the end of their day trip.

Esplanade at Rothesay, 1897. The winter gardens are a delightful feature of the Esplanade and a major attraction for visitors.

Above: Port Bannatyne, Rothesay, 1897. A charming tableau of four children out for a walk along the quayside. From the jetty, boats can be hired for a pleasure trip around the bay.

Above: Esplanade, Rothesay, 1897. A stroll along the Esplanade was a frequent pastime for Victorians. Holiday yachts and pleasure steamers abound.

Left: Port Bannatyne, 1904. Next to Rothesay on the island of Bute, imposing Victorian buildings line the shore of the port, and travel was frequently by boat.

Top: Mount Stuart Village, Rothesay, 1900. A peaceful scene on the idyllic Isle of Bute.

Left: Dumbarton 1897. The famous tea clipper, The Cutty Sark was built in Dumbarton which has a great tradition of shipbuilding. It was also the birthplace of St. Patrick, and it was from here that Mary Queen of Scots sailed to France at the age of six.

Opposite Top: Post Office, Rosneath, 1904. The peaceful village of Rosneath sits on the shores Gare Loch. A mother and daughter pose for the Frith photographer outside the 'Postal Telegraph Office'.

Opposite Below: Clynder, Rosneath, 1906. A pony and trap winds its way up the hill from Rosneath.

HELENSBURGH, nestled at the mouth of the Gare Loch, with its peaceful, wide streets has an air of dignified respectability. This is the birthplace of the inventor of television - John Logie Baird.

Right: Princes Street, Helensburgh, 1901. Looking down Princes Street, the town slopes quietly up from the Clyde affording magnificent views across the river to Greenock.

Above: Helensburgh Esplanade, 1901. Children are having great fun playing on the beach while their parents take a stroll along the esplanade. This was a popular spot for holidaymakers from Glasgow.and for people to keep weekend homes.

Above: Helensburgh, 1901. A peaceful scene showing the wide streets of this residential resort where people came in their small sailing boats from across the Clyde.

Left: Helensburgh, 1901. A nineteenth century Man of War at anchor off Helensburgh.

Opposite Top: Loch Lomond, 1899.
'*Oh, ye'll take the high road, An I'll take the low road, An I'll be in Scotland afore ye, But me an my true love will never meet again On the bonnie, bonnie banks of Loch Lomond.*'

Opposite Below: The Swan Island, Loch Lomond, 1890. The stillness and tranquillity of the loch are highlighted by the mirror like reflections.

Above: Highland Cattle, Loch Long, 1901. A group of magnificent beasts graze unconcernedly on the banks of Loch Long.

Left: Arrochar, 1901. Sitting at the foot of the Arrochar Alps three steamers make ready for their trip down Loch Long and across the Firth.

INVERARAY, home to the Dukes of Argyll since 1701. This small town is the oldest in Argyllshire , but a new town was built on the site of the old in the late eighteenth century. It is best known for its castle built in 1745 after the Dukes had been rewarded for their loyalty to King George II.

Right: Collecting seaweed at Inveraray, 1890. Two crofters gather up baskets of seaweed for use as manure and fertiliser on their small holdings.

Below: Inveraray Castle, 1899. This fine neo-gothic castle sits majestically on the shore of Loch Fyne at the foot of the Argyle hills which sweep off proudly into the distance.

Opposite page: Inveraray, 1899. A mother and son pose by a small fishing boat with the quaint town of Inveraray in the background.

Above: Loch Fyne, Tarbert, 1890. Known for its herring fishing, Tarbert is an attractive little town built around a sheltered bay. In the background you can see the distinctive church that seems to have been built out of proportion to the rest of the town.

Left: Loch Fyne, c 1890. A peaceful scene showing a small peninsula jutting serenely into the loch.

Opposite Top: Arran Castle, c 1890. A group of fishermen take advantage of low tide to catch up on some repairs on their boats.

Opposite Below: Brodick Bay and Castle, Arran, 1890. On the beautiful Isle of Arran you will find the magnificent fortress that is Brodick Castle. Here we can see a couple of fishing boats beached at low tide with the castle in the background.

Left: Iona Abbey, 1903. This wind-swept abbey dates from around 1200. It was a ruin in this photograph, but has since been rebuilt and still attracts pilgrims today.

IONA, "The Cradle of Christianity", only three miles long and one mile wide is the place most people think of when you mention the Hebrides. It was here that Saint Columba set up a monastery in 563 and started to convert the pagan Scots as well as banishing snakes from the island!

Above: Iona, 1903. Fishing boats lay scattered around on the drying seaweed like seals basking in the sun. Although a popular place with tourists, Iona has remained largely unspoilt.

Above: St. Oran's Chapel, Iona, 1903. The chapel, the oldest building on Iona, is said to be the last resting place of many kings including Macbeth and Duncan.

Left: Iona Abbey, 1903. The light glowing through the window of the Abbey ruins produces a very atmospheric scene. It was originally built by the Benedictines in 1200 and was extensively rebuilt in the fifteenth and sixteenth centuries. Since this photograph was taken it has been almost completely restored to its former glory.

WESTERN ISLES. The wild and windy, but stunning landscapes of these bleak islands sustain hardy and somewhat utilitarian villages. The road system was elementary, to say the least, in Frith's day, and has improved little today.

Right: Fingal's Cave, Staffa, 1903. On the romantic, uninhabited island of Staffa you will find awe inspiring caverns cut into the bassalt cliffs. In 1829 the composer Mendelssohn was so inspired by what he saw and heard that he wrote 'Die Fingalsholle', the piece of music that made Fingal's cave famous.

Below: Kyleakin, Isle of Skye, c 1890. This pretty little port is the gateway to Skye from the mainland. It is here that Saucy Mary, a viking princess placed a barrier across the channel and levied a toll from ships sailing through.

Top: The Herring Fleet, Stornoway, 1890. On the island of Lewis, Stornoway is the administrative centre of the Western Isles. The fishing fleet, seen here in harbour prior to another expedition into the Atlantic, is highly important to the prosperity of the people. **Below: The Bay, St. Kilda, 1890.** One of the most westerly of the Western Isles, this picture was taken just forty years before the entire population left the island for good, lured away by the attraction of the outside world and outside money.

ENTRAL SCOTLAND, bridging the Highlands and the Lowlands, has the stunning picturesque scenery of the Trossachs and Loch Lomond. It is the first part of "wild Scotland" to be accessible from the Lowlands. Thus the resort towns became established, and the peaceful lochs and heather clad moors retain their popularity as much today as they did for the Victorians.

Left: Loch Achray, 1871. Rob Roy is said to have been buried above this tranquil loch.

Above: Loch Katrine, 1899. The 'Sir Walter Scott' steams up the loch with another boat load of day trippers immersing themselves in the atmosphere and romance that was the setting for Walter Scott's 'Lady of the Lake'. The loch is more than just a beauty spot, it is the main water supply for Glasgow.

Above: Kilmahog, 1899. This quaint little village is typical of villages to be found in Central Scotland. Showing its strict religious background the house to the right is advertised as having 'temperance refreshments'.

Left: Loch Lubnaig, 1899. Beaching their boat, two holidaymakers enjoy their leisure hours on the beautiful Loch Lubnaig.

CALLANDER. This small burgh is considered the gateway to the Trossachs. Laid out in the eighteenth century, it has long been a popular holiday resort offering traditional Scottish leisure persuits such as good salmon and trout fishing, golf and Highland walks.

Right: Callander viewed from across the River Teith, 1899. Callander lies to the east of the Trossachs and is dominated by Ben Ledi.

Above: Callander main street, 1899. A fine example of early town planning. The town with its wide, sweeping streets was designed and re-built by military architects after the Jacobite rebellion led by Bonnie Prince Charlie.

Above: Callander, 1899. Two lads try a spot of fishing on one of the many rivers in the area that pour down into the River Teith or Loch Lubnaig.

Left: Callander Hydro, 1899. A beautifully proportioned and impressive building which was a focal point for Victorian visitors to the town.

Above: Strathyre, 1899. A tidy well kept little street, reflecting the pride that the people had in their village.

Left: Temperance Hotel, Strathyre, 1901. The residents of the Temperance Hotel enjoy the fine weather sitting and chatting on the front steps.

Opposite Top: Killin, c 1890. Reminiscent of a scene in the Alps, this pretty village sits on the banks of the River Dochart.

Opposite Below: Mill on the Dochart, Killin, 1890. The long exposure of this photograph gives it quite an atmospheric feel, almost like mist rolling over the rocks. The mill is powered by the force of the water which can be quite violent in spring when the snow melts in the mountains and cascades down the rapids and falls.

Right: Head Hotel, Loch Earn, 1899. One of the prestigious hotels that can be found all around this area that is so popular with tourists. The loch is seven miles long and about one mile broad, and is considered to be "singularly attractive, although it is difficult to say exactly wherin lies its charm."

Below: Loch Earn, 1899. At the end of the rickety looking jetty on Loch Earn, a small boy tries to catch some fish whilst his mother looks on.

Above: St. Fillans, 1904.
The houses in this delightful village extend in a long line on the narrow strip between the mountains and the water. A couple stop for a rest during their walk in the foothills of the Grampian mountains.

Left: St. Fillans, 1899. A tranquil view of St. Fillans, situated at the head of Loch Earn, a few miles from Comrie. Saint Fillan, to whom the village owes its name, lived in the eighth century. After being abbot of a monastery on the Holy Loch, he wandered about the West Highlands, buliding churches. He died at Dundern on the other side of Earn from St. Fillans.

Comrie, 1899. Viewed from the east.

COMRIE sits in a picturesque setting along the banks of the River Earn and also lies on the Highland Boundary Fault. This geological location means that Comrie has been subject to more tremors than anywhere else in the British Isles. One of the earliest seismometers in the world is located here in the 'Earthquake House'.

Above: Comrie, 1899. A bicycle leans nonchalantly against the wall while a horse gets a rest on the shady side of the street in this lazy summer setting.

Above: Drummond Street, Comrie, 1904.
The photographer took this wider
angled photograph from further up the
street than the previous view, five years
later. The shopkeeper in the doorway of
Brough and Macpherson appears to have
posed for for the camera.

Left: Comrie, 1899. Viewed from the
bridge across the River Earn, this
pleasant scene shows the little souvenir
and postcard shop. Drummond and Co
the grocers is also featured which would
have stocked Frith photographs.

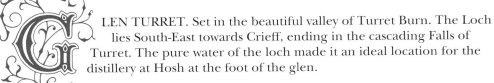

GLEN TURRET. Set in the beautiful valley of Turret Burn. The Loch lies South-East towards Crieff, ending in the cascading Falls of Turret. The pure water of the loch made it an ideal location for the distillery at Hosh at the foot of the glen.

Right: Loch Turret, 1899. The driver of this pony and trap stops to admire the breath taking scenery on his way home.

Below: The Sma' Glen, 1899. The course of the road can easily be seen as it winds its way along the glen into the distance.

Opposite: Grouse Shooting, Glen Turret. Both dog and master together in harmony. You can almost feel the tension and excitement in this picture. Grouse shooting, has for many years, been the sport of the titled and landed gentry.

CRIEFF. Crieff stands on the lower slopes of the Knock which rises to 911 feet, and commands some of the finest views in Scotland. It is said that the name may derive from "Croabh", which is Gaelic for "tree", which may refer to the old gallows tree. Timber from this tree is still preserved in the Town Hall.

Right: James Square, Crieff, 1899. *"Ye lover of the picturesque if ye wish to drown your grief, Take my advice and visit the ancient town of Crieff."* William McGonagall

Above: Comrie Street, Crieff, 1904. Formerly a major cattle market, Crieff really became prosperous when the railway came to town bringing more tourists and their purchasing power. One of Scotland's finest schools, Morrison's Academy, can be found in Crieff.

Top: James Square, Crieff, 1904. A delightfully composed photograph of the attractive street, with some splendid examples of the fashion of the period. **Below: High Street, Crieff, 1899.** Children play in the street unconcerned about the carts trundling past.

Top: Drummond Castle, Crieff, 1899. Two miles south of Crieff, Drummond Castle, founded in 1491, was badly damaged in the Civil War. Only the tower now remains. Frith's photograph depicts a splendid vista of the castle's famed Italian sunken garden.
Below: Monzie Castle, Crieff, 1899. Monzie Castle also suffered extensive damage - but in this case from fire. It was rebuilt in the early nineteen hundreds, so the photograph must have been taken before the fire.

Top: Muthill, 1899. Three miles south of Crieff lies the small town of Muthill. The name Muthill is derived from Moot-Hill meaning hill of meeting. Here a little girl gazes intently at the camera, shielding her eyes..

Left: Muthill, 1899. Two rather dour looking housewives look at the photographer with distrust.

BAN. The coming of the railway to Oban in 1880 made it a popular resort with the Victorians. It became known as the new "Charing Cross of the Highlands" as it was then possible to take trips to the surrounding islands and sea lochs. Built round a sheltered bay, the natural setting is superb.

Previous page: Sound of Kerrera, 1903. Sheltering Oban from the worst the weather can throw at it, the island of Kerrera stands defiantly across the bay.

Right: George Street, Oban, 1901. A plethora of fine hotels with magnificent views across to the island of Kerrera.

Below: Oban Bay, 1901. Various craft bob up and down in the bay which enjoys the benefit of natural shelter from Kerrera, making Oban an ideal place in which to take a sailing holiday.

Connel Ferry Bridge, 1903. A fine example of Victorian engineering.

Loch Shiel, 1890. The Glenfinnan Monument rises above the marshy ground at the northern end of Loch Shiel. Built to commemorate the raising of Prince Charlie's standard it is crowned with a statue of an unknown Highlander.

LEN COE. Set in the valley of the River Coe, with the small village of Glencoe at the foot of the glen, the tranquillity in these photographs form a strong contrast to its bloody history.

Right: The scene of the massacre, Glencoe, 1890. Probably the most dishonourable act in Scotland's violent history took place here in 1692. After accepting the hospitality of MacDonald of Glencoe, Robert Campbell rose early in the morning, and with his soldiers, massacred 38 of their hosts. This act was sanctioned by the government of the time as a way of ridding themselves of any potential threat from the powerful MacDonald clan. Even today feelings run deep between the MacDonalds and the Campbells.

Below: Glencoe, 1899. These quaint, thatched, crofters cottages are typical of those found dotted all over the Highlands.

Above: Inverlochy, In this picturesque location stands the ruins of Inverlochy Castle, the site of several bloody battles.

Left: Ben Nevis viewed from Corpach, 1890. The mighty Ben Nevis dominates the skyline in this powerful picture. At 4406 feet, Ben Nevis is Britain's highest mountain.

HIGHLANDS. Covering two thirds of the country, Scotland's Highlands, while sparsely populated, have some of the most fabulous scenery - mountains and glens, lochs and rivers, majestic coastlines and rugged moorland. Travel must have presented a formidable challenge to Francis Frith, yet the photographs bear witness to his success.

Right: Ben Eay, 1890. A crofters cottage sits exposed to the elements as the crofters struggle to make ends meet in this harsh existence.

Glen Affric, c 1890. A rickety foot bridge crosses the river, presenting an idyllic view downstream.

Above: Flowerdale, Gairloch, 1890. This lovely little stone bridge provides a perfect focal point to the picture as it carries the road to the sturdy stone built houses.

Left: Falls of Rogie, 1890. An impossibly beautiful spot set in the midst of trees and heather where salmon attempt to leap the falls to reach their spawning grounds upstream.

Above: Inverness, from the castle, c 1890. Spanning the River Ness, the Ness Bridge, as seen from the castle, is a magnificent suspension bridge joining the two halves of Inverness.

Left: Culloden House, c 1880. Set in beautifully kept grounds, the house stands as a reminder of an age long gone.

Opposite top: Strathpeffer, c 1890. Two girls are hard at work dyeing lengths of linen.

Opposite below: Dingwall, 1890. Once a busy port this market town is best known for being the birth place of Macbeth, king of Scotland from 1040 - 1057.

Right: Cawdor Castle, 1890. Said to be where the three witches once told Macbeth that he was soon to become Thane of Cawdor and then king. All this came true but three hundred years before this castle was built.

Below: Forres viewed from the breakwater, 1890. It is rumoured that not far from here Macbeth met the witches on his way to Forres, where King Duncan held court.

Above: Elgin, 1890. Flanked by fine examples of Victorian architecture these four men pose for a photograph. You will see that one of them is balancing a tray on his head that seems to hold a loaf of bread.

Left: Herring boats, Fraserburgh, 1900. The famous herring fleet of Fraserburgh. Even today the economy of the town relies heavily on fishing.

Following Page: Herring boats, Fraserburgh, 1900. The herring fleet ties up and prepares for another trip to the wild waters of the Atlantic.

A BERDEEN .The Granite City, so called because of its 'grey' granite architecture, has always been a major centre for trade. Because of its geographical location it has made an ideal port for exports of granite, paper and textiles. The famous Aberdeen Clippers revolutionised sea transport, but with the introduction of steam in 1882, trawlfishing became the new industry.

Right: Aberdeen, c 1885. Industrial Aberdeen, with its skyline pock marked by chimney stacks and its air polluted by smoke, is seen as a backdrop to a fine Victorian suspension bridge.

Above: Aberdeen, c 1885. Looking down Castle Gate towards Marischal College which, with its ornate decorations, is the second largest granite building in the world.

Above: Market Cross (Mercat Cross), Aberdeen, 1892. The cross, with its wonderful carvings of the Stuart monarchs, used to be the main meeting place in Aberdeen. People would meet here to trade goods and gossip (a valuable commodity).

Left: Brig O'Balgownie, Aberdeen, c 1890. The Brig O'Balgownie is the oldest medieval bridge in Scotland and spans the River Don. Its high gothic arch gives it a distinctive shape and allows larger boats to pass beneath it.

Above: Mill on the Clunie, Braemar, 1890. Beside the fast flowing Clunie the natural force of the water is harnessed to power this mill.

Left: Cairnwell, Braemar, 1879. Before the introduction of snowploughs, it all had to be cleared by hand.

Opposite top: The coast at Muchalls, 1890. This beautiful rocky coastline can be quite dangerous to the uninitiated, as many sailors have found to their cost.

Opposite below: Dunnottar Castle, c 1900. In what is undoubtably one of the most awe-inspiring locations for a castle, Dunnottar sits 160 feet above the waves on an easily defendable promontory.

Left: Stirling, 1899.

STIRLING sits on the River Forth, a town steeped in history, its castle was home to such romantic figures as King Arthur, Mary Queen of Scots and James V. Less than two miles from here was fought the great and bloody battle of Bannockburn where Robert the Bruce defeated the English troops in 1314.

Above: Broad Street, Stirling, 1899. A town where many historical events have taken place, including the coronation of Mary Queen of Scots. Broad street was the site of the market place and centre of the medieval town. Damley House, at the bottom of the street, is reputed to be the lodging house of the said Mary Queen of Scots.

Above: Bridge of Allan, 1899. A pleasant little spa town with neat tidy streets.

Left: Bridge and Cathedral, Dunblane, 1899. Famous for its cathedral, which was founded in 600, Dunblane occupies an attractive spot in the valley of the Allan Water.

A BERDOUR. The famous "silver sands" of Aberdour on the south coast of Fife were an attraction to Victorian holidaymakers, but the icy east wind meant that the leisure pursuits were more active than the name may have suggested.

Previous page: Stone Pier, Aberdour, 1900. Passengers embark on a ferry for a trip across the Firth of Forth.

Right: Aberdour, 1897. The ferry departs from the quay. The paddle steamer was revolutionary at the time this photograph was taken, a novelty for the passengers.

Above: Aberdour High Street, 1900. Although a popular holiday resort, Victorian attire was no doubt an advantage against the 'bracing' winds.

Above: Woodside Hotel, Aberdour, 1900. A wagon unloads its luggage for the hotel guests.

Left: Inchcolm, 1900. Situated on a tiny little island of Inchcolm in the Firth of Forth stands the Abbey of St. Columba

PERTH was, until the middle of the 15th century, the capital of Scotland, and is still the capital of the Highlands today. Perth is placed where it is because it is at the easiest fording place of the River Tay. It has a long history as a livestock trading centre, and expanded in the eighteenth century to become a finance centre.

Right: Post Office and New Scott Street, Perth, 1899. The busy Post Office would be a life line for businesses in Perth that had to contact other cities around the country.

Below: High Street West, Perth, 1899. A very busy street scene, the two little girls seem to be fascinated by the goods in the cart on the left.

Above: Bridge and Monument, Perth, 1899. It was quite common to see children running around in bare feet, such as these in the park in Perth. But it was quite rare to see them without a cap or hat on.

Left: High Street East, Perth, 1899. These children seem totally unconcerned about the approaching horse drawn tram as they stand chatting in the street..

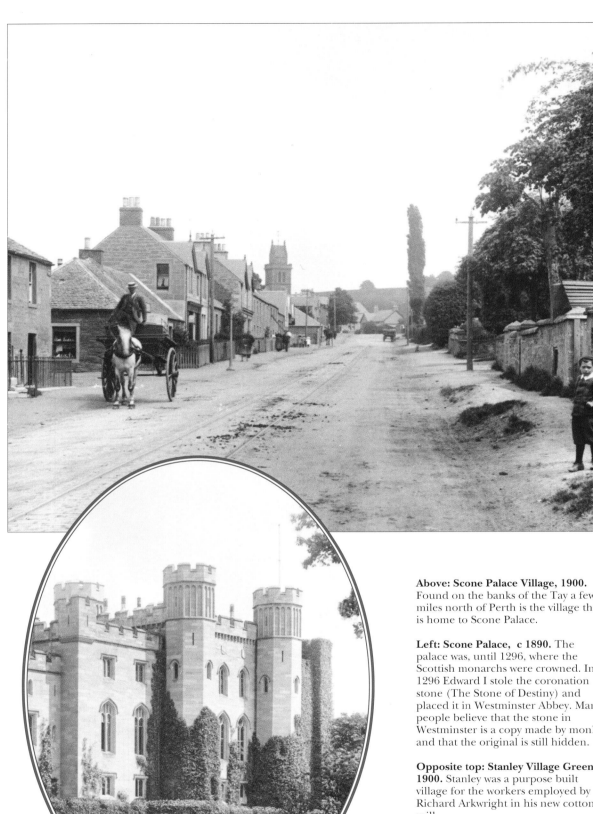

Above: Scone Palace Village, 1900. Found on the banks of the Tay a few miles north of Perth is the village that is home to Scone Palace.

Left: Scone Palace, c 1890. The palace was, until 1296, where the Scottish monarchs were crowned. In 1296 Edward I stole the coronation stone (The Stone of Destiny) and placed it in Westminster Abbey. Many people believe that the stone in Westminster is a copy made by monks and that the original is still hidden.

Opposite top: Stanley Village Green, 1900. Stanley was a purpose built village for the workers employed by Richard Arkwright in his new cotton mill.

Opposite below: Stanley viewed from Duchess Street, 1900. The quaint cottages flank the street as it slopes away into the distance.

Right: Kirriemuir, c 1890. This small, attractive town is the birthplace of J.M.Barrie, the author of Peter Pan. It was from this romantic background that he invented his characters for one of the best childrens books ever written.

Below: Kirriemuir High Street, c 1890. It seems impossible that any horse could pull such a heavily loaded cart. The cart is laden down with chairs, pans, etc, the trappings of a travelling pedlar.

Above: Alexandra Fountain, Dundee, 1907. Dundee's main claim to fame is that Captain Scott's ship, Discovery, was built here for his expedition to the Antarctic.

Left: Bankfoot village, 1900. These solidly built stone cottages would keep out the worst of the Scottish weather.

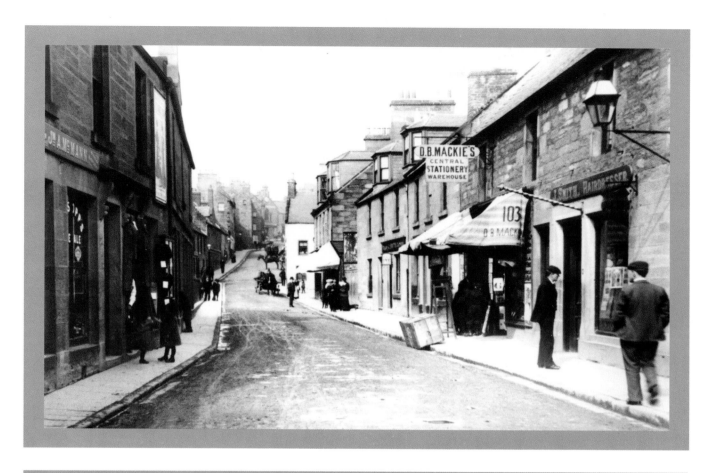

Opposite: St. David Street, Brechin, 1900. A charming tableau of children on their way to school. Note the smart the pinafores and boaters.
Top: High Street, Brechin, 1900. This pretty little town boasts an unusual round tapered tower, one of only two in mainland Scotland.
Below: Drumtochty, 1899. This charming village is captured here on a lovely summers day where people are out for a stroll.

K BULL LODGINGS for TRAVELLERS & WORKING MEN. 12.

THE BEEHIVE INN

EDINBURGH. Dominated by its spectacular castle perched high up on its volcanic block, has provided the inspiration for many writers and artists, both Sir Walter Scott and Robert Louis Stevenson have strong links with the city. Edinburgh has always been a lively city full of charm and beauty, with diverse architectural styles and a variety of cultures.

Previous page: Edinburgh castle viewed from Grassmarket, 1897. A superb view of the majestic castle which dominates the capital city.

Right: Princes Street West End, 1897. An image which encapsulates the bustle of *the* shopping street in Victorian Edinburgh

Above: John Knox's house, Edinburgh, 1897. Knox, the protestant reformer, gained a reputation as a charismatic preacher during his turbulent life within the church. It is believed that Knox died in this house after a lifetime of preaching hellfire and eternal damnation.

Above: St. Giles' Cathedral, Edinburgh, 1897. The birth place of the Scottish Reformation is officially called' The High Kirk of St. Giles' but is more often referred to as a cathedral.

Left: Museum of Antiquities, 1897. This imposing building also houses the Scottish National Portrait Gallery. It contains the most comprehensive collection of the social history of Scotland from the Stone Age. It was founded in 1781 by the Society of Antiquaries of Scotland with the aim of attracting antiquities from all over the world, but in time the emphasis changed to the collection of Scotish artefacts. Note the immaculately turned out horses and carriages waiting for patrons of the museum.

Above: Princes Street, Edinburgh, 1897. Built on one side only, to reveal unobstructed views of the castle, Princes Street is Edinburgh's most famous thoroughfare.

Left: Princes Street, Edinburgh, 1890. Another view of the Scott Monument, this time from the busy Princes Street.

Opposite top: Black watch on the castle esplanade, 1897. So called because of their dark tartan and their dedication to keeping watch over the highlands.

Opposite below: Cannongate Tollbooth, 1897. This extraordinary building with its distinctive turrets and protruding clock make this a familiar landmark.

Right: Newhaven Harbour, 1897. The deep water anchorage of Newhaven made this an ideal place for large shipbuilding in the 16th century, but today it is now a quiet little fishing port with attractive little boats bobbing on the water.

Below: Fishermen's cottages, Newhaven, 1897. These utilitarian terraced cottages are home to the fishermen and their families. The hard way of life has toughened these people but has not destroyed their sense of humour and loyalty in this close knit community.

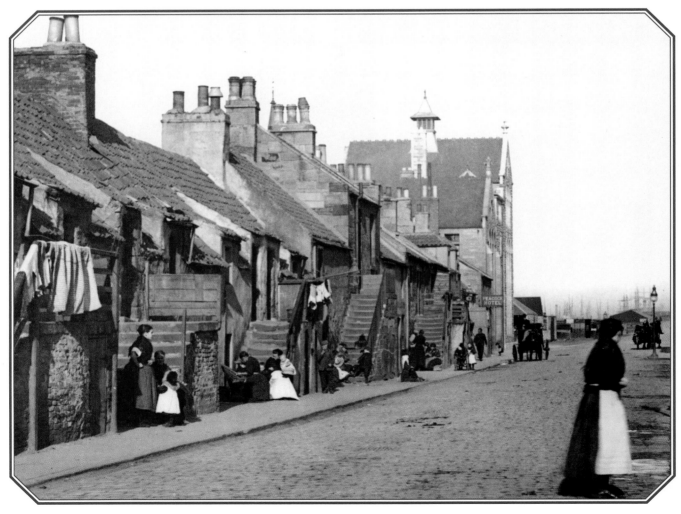

Above: Forth Bridge, 1897. Pictured here effortlessly spanning the Firth of Forth, this is undoubtably one of the most famous bridges in the world. Painting it has become synonymous with seemingly never ending tasks..

Left: Linlithgow Palace viewed from the Boat Station, 1897. Birthplace of Mary Queen of Scots, the palace is perched in a beautiful setting on the banks of Linlithgow Loch.

Right: Roslin Chapel, 1897. Parts of this highly decorated fifteenth century chapel feature some of the most exquisite carvings to be found in this country.

Above: Quality Street, North Berwick, 1897. A well composed photograph which shows the wonderful diversity of architectural styles to be found in the area in Frith's day. No doubt there are some less attractive additions to mar the outlook today.

Top: Gilmerton, 1899. A group of 'little rascals' pose for a picture as they play on the side of the dusty road. Note one little tike determined not to be recognised, by covering his face.
Below: Gilmerton, 1899. An idyllic little village captured here on a sleepy summer afternoon.

Index